They Gather Around Me, the Animals

They Gather Around Me, the Animals

⁊

Kunjana Parashar

Selected by Diane Seuss as winner
of the 2024 Barbara Stevens Poetry Book Award

National Federation of State Poetry Societies

Editing by Eleanor Berry
Cover design and interior layout by Shawn Aveningo Sanders (The Poetry Box)
NFSPS emblem: Owl of Athena from ancient Athenian tetradrachm coin
Book set in Adobe Garamond Pro
Cover images sourced and licensed via Envato.com
Author photograph by Prerna Parashar
These images are used with permission. Copyright to all images is retained by the artists.

ISBN: 979-8-9929766-0-1

Published June 2025
NFSPS Press

JUDGE'S COMMENT

The brilliance of Kunjana Parashar's *They Gather Around Me, the Animals* gleams through the lens of the majesty of the animals that were here, are here, and may well be disappearing, in poems jubilant and elegiac at once. Parashar's approach to language and form evolves through the course of the book, from the devotional to the surreal, from contrapuntal to pantoum, concrete poems to erasures, poems written in both the presence and the absence of the animals that are their subjects, and written in a diction which opens the lexicon to the language of the ecological imagination. "i see pictures of blue-green hexacorals / patching a floor of zoanthids like a zardozi dream / & i say listen, i love you too," she writes. Parashar's speaker is "never not listening," and never not watching, and she listens to and watches the actual world, not the world as sifted through a screen. Thus, she knows that "[w]hales slap on the coast like fingers on guitars." That "[n]ow that the birds are gone, we hang our cuckoo clocks upside down." That rain falls "like a bag of teeth on tin roofs." That in the absence of birds, "[w]e break our binoculars in grief." That in the absence of howls, in a poem without dogs, "we lost our vowel sounds." How the lyric itself, the music of our consonants and vowels, is contingent upon the voices of animals.

Diane Seuss
author of *frank: sonnets*
and *Modern Poetry*

CONTENTS

Dedication

To pollen. To gadfly. Beetle of red.
Green crown of leaf. To strawberries.
And mulch. Squelchy soles of boots.
To bogs. To the ancients who live in them.
To neelakurinji. To golden-backed frogs
in the ghats. To sleet. And
sulphur. To samudra phool. To mitti.
To the rain that brings hail. To civets.
To palm toddy. To bees. To aphids.
To lac bugs on a kusum tree. To fleas.
Spider legs. Blizzard. Sundogs
and puddles. To winter light and
its simple oppression. Gold of scarabs.
Hermaphrodite snail. The eyes of eels.

Prayer

-after Louise Glück

I'll tell you how I spend my time.
I walk on this earth,
a bangle of green. I spend
hours by the rocks where
the water flows in squirts
and insects scheme against grass.
I seem quiet in the way of stones
but I am never not listening: in fact
I'm looking for some evidence
that I am no more than a small thing
clogged among smaller beings,
that I am moving, and a snake
is as alive as me breathing
in the deep scent of soil
upon which the rain has drummed
its black chorus of clouds.
I dig my hands into the dark sleep of moss.
As shineless now as the first sunspot.
Yes. These are the signs
I've been looking for.

Wait

If you find yourself unfed
and kneeling by the rocks on the beach
not to look for a hermit crab
or a sea-slug in the intertidal zone

but hunched in pain and crying over
an errand, a boy or a broken heel, do not bristle
at the excess of spring.

Do not wish the leaves off trees.

Wait for the mesic soils to turn.
The westerlies to come.
Watch the koels go from being shy
to shagging loudly in the berried bushes.

Wait.

Old-World vultures will survive.
Everywhere will be chameleons and bees.

And all the limp Mexican salamanders,
        those mighty little axolotls,
will regrow their small feet.

I'd like to shun this world

but how can I
when I know of the yucca moth
that pollinates the yucca plant
and if you took away the moth
or if you took away the yucca flowers
they would die
each without the other
and it is for miracles like these
that I think there is a God,
that I believe in the sun
when it wakes up every morning
and spreads its strobing light around,
that I believe in the goodness of odd numbers
and the silkiness of silkworms
and this is why
even on the most desolate day
I try to look for the leaf-insect
hiding in the clear green of leaves
like dew upon a raindrop,
or think of the million wild horses
that have yet to run
with perfect and imperfect hooves
among all the tall necks
of all the tall grasses.

what are you, an environmentalist?
or a love letter to mumbai's intertidal zone

everything comes and goes, repeat the priests
of scriptures, gnostic & unwavering.
i am not that wise, o tiny sea-slug,
sacoglossan green. i take things to heart.
more like the moon, you know? maybe
that's why i love you without having studied you.
i see pictures of blue-green hexacorals
patching a floor of zoanthids like a zardozi dream
& i say listen, i love you too. yes, call me
your vast mother, for i'll be sad
to see you go (tarred by a road).
it's true i don't understand much. what
the word empirical really means. why plankton
start to glow. how aquifers empty.
but love does not need a gaunt theorem
to explain it. *love loves*, as the ones
with an odd grammar in the conch of their ear say
to make a thing doubly secure, a love
so luminous it rights the wrong, *irregardless*.
and so i repeat, before it all goes,
i love you, my sweet bombil.
i love you, my anemone.

The Garden

I do not think you more special, more skilled.
Everything is filled with multiplication—
with the math of want. The pulp of desire
rises like sap in the crotch of trees. Snails
pass a luminous dart of sperm from
one open part to another—500 eggs a year,
if numbers mean anything at all.
And for whom do you think
the frogs croak a nightly chorus
of rainsong, sacs
bulging with sex? You'd best believe
this tameness of grass is a lie.
You'd best believe we are not
the only ones in the garden tonight.

Invocation

It has come. The hour of slow loris.
Thrush, rat, night heron.
The hour of bat excrement. The gift of guano.
Rich mineral dropped in a lake.
Deep wells of ore. Nitrogenous rock cave.
Erect forms have turned fetal, embryonic again.
And the waters shine silver with the sleep
of a million sardines. It is time.
Awake, cricket. Awake, cereus. Bear and
honey badger, awake. Mark the air
with your solitary cry, o wolf, hyena,
purple frog. It is your hour. To you it belongs,
all of earth, the dark, luscious sap of plants,
the moonlit wriggle of worms, tall shadows
of pine, fig, acacias, khejri, the hollong.
Palm civets, come out. Out of the cover
of cement-drains, out of the tubs lined with
mucus, out of your scared, arboreal stupor.
No more the tedious hum of radiators.
No more the loud earth-masters quarrying rock,
soil, stone. It is yours, the mulch, the ooze,
the cool and silent tomb of the underground.
Returned to you for the night, the dark ball of earth.
Play with it, o fishing cat. Have your fill
of shimmering koi from unmanned office ponds.
Awake, tuberoses. Awake, drowsy pods
of mogra. Sweet shiuli, awake. Scent
all orifices with your nightly bouquet.

What I planted under the hydrangeas

remained hidden. I didn't know then
what those shrubs were called. Only that
the flowerheads were a strange sort
of cluster. Something to do
with water in the name. The thing
was buried at least three feet deep.
You'd think a girl couldn't manage
that on her own but my arms
are like my mother's and my palms
can thwack the hardiest of cheeks.
I do not boast of it and yet it's true.
What was the thing? I do not
remember. Only that it stank
like a dead cat by the lakeside,
a mix of algae & DDT.
I could tell, for the vulture died
the same way. But it wasn't
a cat, was it? It was something
else, rotten and shrunken like
a piece of the earth sucked
dry of any water or nutrient,
barren and foul. Perhaps
the shape was feline. Yes,
that could be it. Boney
and dark. Dark as owls'
yellow eyes. Yellow is bright,
but it can be dark. The hydrangeas
bloomed clean over the buried thing.
Blue cabbage florets on
their heads. You see,
the picture didn't suggest
crime but beauty. Frothing
like the white of full moons.
Nobody knew what I had done.
What grew underneath.

The Great Yawn

Something like a great yawn is coming.

We rub our soles,
we glue our feet.

Like an egg cracking over the sky, yolk dripping on our bald heads.

We pin up temperature records,
we hide from the heat.

Oil floats on bogs like a queen on a barge.

We reduce our hunger,
we ready our fleets.

Whales slap on the coast like fingers on guitars.

We sharpen our torsos
and load up on batteries.

An extinction of hogs, an extinction of snakes.

We look for more land,
we dig up all the seas.

Like a bible full of warts, we watch frogs fall from the trees.

We shuffle our cards,
we pray to the god of concrete.

The Glitch

When it began to melt—the thin membrane between all worlds animal & human—shoals of dead fish washed ashore. It was like a glitch or several meridians malfunctioning. Something geographical, something big. We did all sorts of things to survive. We wrestled the teeth out of eels. We stole the bones from the mouths of adjutant storks. From the combs and colonies, we took ounces of honey. There was no use to candle our way out of grief. What we needed was meat. Mountains of it. What we needed was water. Fresh water, even sleet. Something that had once protected us, once watched over us, seemed to have gone to sleep. Was God a conked-out machine? There was no time to think. It all seemed empty or late, our hemispheres of guilt, our ideas of fate. We donned our animal masks & waited for the next kill.

Poem with Dead Birds in It

only   commas   crowd   the sky

  we look   upon   the butchered   bodies

    (shikra   hawk   eagle

        jacana   auk   tit)

        we whistle   chirp

           quaver

our   compasses   shaking   wildly

  (crow   tragopan   starling

    pitta   vulture   lapwing)

      every-   where   over

    lakes   trees   pondwater   sea-links

          a litany of feathers

      dead   things

In the Zoo

In the zoo, the animals are either manic or deadly calm. Stag humps the cutout of a doe in his cage. Heron sits monklike on a drawing of a pond. In the fishing zone, no fish remain. Tiger paces the cardboard enclave. Beavers make a dam out of slime. In the place of dogs, more wolf-like cutouts. Somewhere on the top, a banner reads: 'Today on display: a gharial's snout, an axolotl's tail, a yellownape's feather, a rhino's hide.' A child asks, Crocodile, crocodile, may we cross your river? Only if you are wearing grey, the crocodile replies. Grey? Yes, like the asphalt, like the ash into which a forest burns. What's happening to the animals? someone asks in a high-pitched voice. What's happening? we repeat, like the faces of dolls melting in a house fire. Where is the zookeeper? we ask each other, speech garbled in panic. The children ask, Where is the krait, where is the star tortoise? Who has the keys, we ask, where is the gate?

The Creature

At first it was restless, then it turned gentle. Like a cat god appeased with a lunch of mice. It grew a little each time we fed it, like a plant, a carnivorous thing. We thought we'd flung it from the terrace. We thought we were free. We were wrong. Sphagnum and cold water bubbled from the fridge. It grew heavy as a flower that could eat a 4-foot child. We got our buckets ready, tin and plastic, attached long poles to squeegees. It felt like a murder we couldn't hide except it wasn't a murder. It was nothing like one. It was like a dream. Fragrant and clean. Pus oozed from its seams. Did I say it was clean? I meant clean with fluid. Clean with wounds on its pocked body. The odor, I imagined—no, I smelled— was of dung beetles, small but fruity. Does that make sense? we asked each other. *Does that make sense?* But each of us felt quiet so we thought to let it be. We hacked at the body fruiting with berries and pinched the pustules growing on its feet. How did it walk with such pain? How did it swim? How did its feet find their way to our doorstep? Why did we let it in? Although it didn't speak, we didn't think language was enough to communicate. We spoke in incomplete gestures, in mime, in sighs and squeaks. Like an animal to a woman. Like a man to a man. Never saying the thing but skirting to reach there. So much better than words, the manner of body. Leaking with liquid, leaking with a dungy smell, limbs easy to hold and hoick. We yanked its hair like weeds. Like I said, it had turned gentle. It wouldn't bite us. We'd robbed it of its teeth.

Poem with No Birds in It

Now that the birds are gone, we hang our cuckoo clocks upside down. Insects yawp and trill from windshields and kitchen sinks. The sun still comes out blaring like a red horn, but the pheasants are nil. On the mountains, in the eaves, under awnings, on ficuses, not one blasted wing. In the skies, a mass migration of dragonflies. In our hands, just the rattle of leftover casques and bills like souvenirs from a past so long ago but so near. No more cocks announcing the coming of light, no more frogmouths signalling the arrival of night. Styes grow on the eyes of trees. We break our binoculars in grief.

Poem with No Dogs in It

When the dogs were gone, they left behind no song of barks. Dog owners pulled at the leash, but no one pulled back. There was no exchange. Just an absence of form. Like Canis Major missing from the sky. Everywhere we went we found empty jowls, rotten teeth, piles of bare ribs. But in the lack of fur, the ticks were nowhere to be found. Now that they could not eat the pariahs, leopards emerged from the fringes of the city and entered our gated colonies. We roamed with torches in our hands and fires ablaze. Keelbacks swam in the blackwaters near town. Not just our pets, the dholes were gone too from the ghats. We searched in the dark but there was no god to be found. Our hands missed the grip of muzzles, the pliancy of cocked ears, the watch of tilted gaze. It was a missing of gigantic proportions. We raised statues of canines from cardboard, from clay, from the long jaw of memory. Days passed without howls. One by one we lost our vowel sounds.

Poem with No Birdsong in It

Instead, a hammering of nails. Wedges snapping in two. Machine parts welding into more machine parts. Bricks being loaded into lorries. Chopped wood rattling like bones in the backs of vans. Blasters blasting the innards of earth. Shots fired from Diwali cracker guns. From the insides of trucks, the fall of molten tar blacker than crows. The clatter of a hundred TMT bars in the backs of 18-chakka trucks. Drills louder than peckers drilling holes to hang photos and ID cards. Excavators quarrying rocks; bucketing tubers, claw, soil, nutrients, star. In our food, more chewable gravel. From our lips, no whistle, only the clack & chirr of mechanical mouthparts.

Poem with an Absence of Snakes

One night, we found their skins everywhere like a secret ripped open—across the metro stations, on the cell towers, under classroom desks. Just a long skein of scales scattered across the tekdi. But there was no hiss in the grass, no hiss in the air. Where had they been and where were they going gliding like ribbons in the dark, bodies slick and nude like a newborn's head? What was it we felt? We had never been close. In fact, we were afraid of them. We hunted them with sticks, the snakes. Why, then, this desire to see them up close now that they were gone? What was this missing in the soul? We weren't herpetologists. We were certainly not friends. It was unknown to us in what tunnels and down what holes they lived and sought their prey. Was it like the ache of losing a language and so a whole culture? Was every species that way? we wondered as we dug their graves.

Poem Where We Never See the Light of Day

No sun. It is blacker than a crow. Blacker than most stilettos. Blacker than sinkholes. A black we have never seen. A black we cannot conceive. A black beyond black beyond black. Dark as the sheet of tar melting on the road. Dark as the holes through which no light passes. Dark as blackcurrants in a black bowl. Like seeing through the dark eye of a whale or a needle and looking at nothing. Darker than space. Did we mention the crow? We meant carrion crow, sing heigh-ho, fol de riddle, lol de riddle, hi ding do.

Poem with No Plants in It

(a burning haibun)

Lumps of coal. Brick & sand. From the earth, spades and gardening forks coming up empty. Where was once sap, once chloroplast, once sugar, once moist, now is only xeric soil. We weep a small weep. The sun chortles bright, burns everything with the scope to leaf. Even the strongest of roots will not take. How to propagate what does not exist? Snatch from what garden a snake plant, some cumbersome vine? It'll be fine, we tell our children. Go to sleep. Oh, where is the green fuse? Where is the flower? We weep a small weep. Don't let the children see. Our hands are empty as rakes.

//

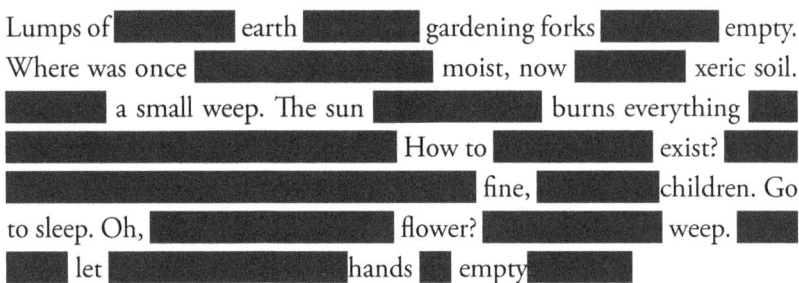

Lumps of ███████ earth ███████ gardening forks ███████ empty. Where was once ███████████ moist, now ████████ xeric soil. ██████ a small weep. The sun ██████████ burns everything ███ ██████████████████ How to █████████ exist? █████ ██████████████████████████ fine, ████████ children. Go to sleep. Oh, ██████████████ flower? ████████████ weep. ███ ████ let ████████████ hands ██ empty████████

//

██████ earth █████████████████████████████████ ██████████████████████████ how exist? ████████████████████ oh, ██████ weep. ████████████████

Poem with Fire Everywhere

The snow was on fire. Old trees caught fire. Fire tickled the bellies of whales and tardigrades. It blazed through the dreams of sleeping fish. Whatever we thought could never burn was licked by fire. The ocean grew an eye of fire. It was in the bells of temples and the spires of monuments. A long tongue of fire. Children scrawled hot letters onto slates. A deeply ashen face towered over us like a giant cumulonimbus. We couldn't believe its size and power. How little it was at first, the fire, how far from where we lived, how far from the places we called ours. But that was our first mistake. Everything had been ours.

Poem with an Invasive Species in It

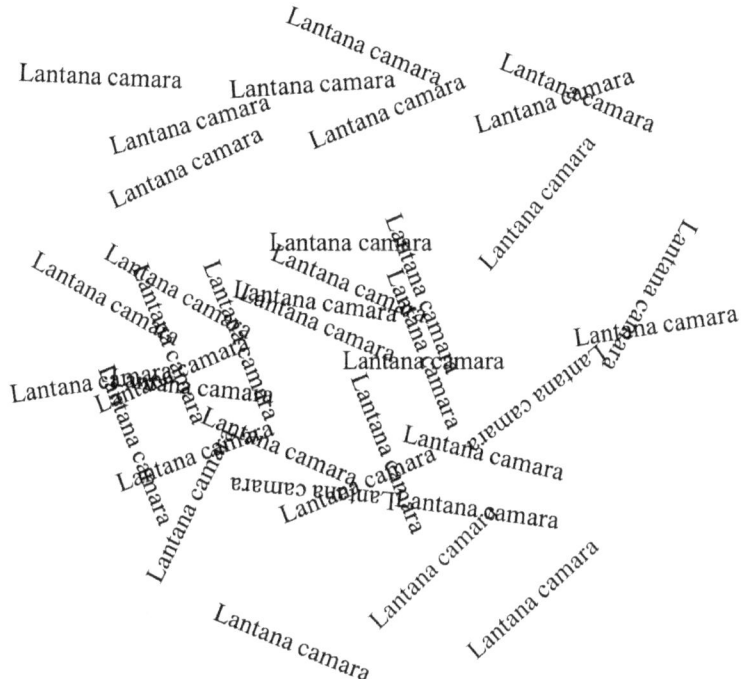

Poem with No [   ] in It

[   ] left in 2029. It was unceremonious. Simple as a surgical stitch on the arm. No five-pointed star blinked in the sky. In the air, not a single string of a mourning harp. Half of us couldn't even tell what use the [   ] had been. Nor the make or function, the color or scent. Perhaps the sight of [   ] was pretty. Yes, perhaps. It wasn't necessary for building bridges or laying bricks. It didn't leave so much as a tear, let alone a scar. Much earlier, they'd gawk at the arrival of [   ]. In fact, they'd wait all year for the seasons to turn, especially the lovers and the poets. They, who were once us. But now we can't remember the form of [   ]. Whether it had a face or a heart. A tail or a premonition. What beckoned it to leave or if it came to any harm. The hours are gaunt. Our lips hurt from the cold and the heat. We take what we can. Even if it costs an arm.

Yellow Rubber Duckies

We kept them stuffed in an old bin, but the yellow rubber duckies multiplied like the offspring of horny pigeons. They flowed out of the bin and into the kitchen sink. Soon they were in the drain pipes. Then in the sea, and in the ocean currents, and in our food. An army of them. A bright yellow army. A fleet. Slowly but surely, yellow rubber duckies overtook the fish & the sharks. Seagulls started to squawk yellow syllables in the dark. Our babies came out rubbery & odd, squealing like piglets. We tried to drown the duckies, but we could not. They came back up like immortal cockroaches. And so we knelt, naked and wet, before our new gods.

The Forgetting

Everything was out of joint. We tried to memorize what was going, what would be gone: the tooth of a megalodon, the horns of an urial, the legs of a godwit. Already we had begun to lose the shapes of animals. Already the birds were wingless and bald. When it started to get worse, our clocks broke down. Our alphabets sounded funny, our voices small. Like the slow, automatic hand of a machine, we began to sputter and to speak with a drawl. It grew more rapid, the forgetting of our stories and songs. So we sat our children down. We forced them to muscle their brains and hands to make origami rain and origami frogs. *Someone must remember*, we repeated into the small conches of their ears. *Someone must write it down.*

Afterwaters

When the water came, I let my body go.
   My lungs became accordions.

I bellowed blue music from my many pores.
   Could they hear me,

bubbling from below, the fish?
   Did my song reach their earstones?

I sank low in the aphotic zone.
   What good was the blue mass of my body?

But as if I were whalefall, they gathered
   around me, the animals.

Anglerfish-breath & fanged-tooth.
   Scores of segmented worms gnaw-

ed my foot. Mussels and squids
   trailed across my belly.

Light-bulbed ctenophores
   waved past my breast.

In life, there was more of me.
   But in death, I felt full.

Swimming Upstream

When the air will heat, the snow trout
will leave the low-altitude Himalayan rivers.

They will push upwards—to the colder waters.
Squeeze together in their rush to survive.

A habitat is like a home. A habitat is a home.
If you lose a home, impermanence becomes natural. Easy.

I was always on the third floor. When things got hot,
I was pushed out. Now I live on the seventh floor.

A learned slimming of comforts is often a virtue.
To trudge, to travel up, is to prepare the body for the final leaving.

For now, this rented apartment overlooks a hill.
Tomorrow, there may be no hill to orient toward—

Where, then, to hang the sun?

How to calm the snow globe shaken into vertigo,
the flakes flung into glycerine space like a panic of birds?

I'll reset the directions—bony skyscrapers, east.
Tarpaulin-roofed shanties honeycombed in west.

Noisy neighbours to my south.
North, some homeless fish.

Diapause

To sleep. To be a leaky tugboat anchored on the water,
resting gently. To resist breaking into new growth—
this infinite croak of progress, all talk of brick & mortar.

To accept the suspended offspring. Pupa not mothed.
Wings undeveloped. Body small. Not worm enough for a beak.
Not to applaud the little green shoot pushing out from concrete.

Not to see it as hope, but as a thing that couldn't help
take root, now rotting—to honor this death, to let
children go. The embryo unmade. An image erased.

The whoosh of baby static empty like air blades.
All sound gone beyond the transducer's sonar beam.

A sleep. A deep sleep of substratum, a diapause.
An arribada cut short by the swoop of black caws.

Sweet shoal of fish stilled in a caiman's dream.

Afterwards

I woke with a start. Like a bell whose tongue had been asleep for years, now suddenly cast into music. I gargled the damp air. I was a forest. Of course I was. Maggots feasted on the rump of a dead horse. Everything eats, was my first real thought. My feet felt like a tree that hadn't moved in years, roots clinging to the udder of the earth. My dreams felt fungal. Stemless mushrooms grew on my calves. When I yawned, birds flew out from the O of my mouth. Deer mewled like little rats. Everywhere was fern.

Green Bottle Flies

When the pigeon died and rotted close to an old rubber tire by the compound gate, the green bottle flies came. Battling the tongues of frogs, battling the webs of hidden spiders, they came, the bottle flies, green metal shine on their backs. I'd only ever seen them in sweetmeat shops, hovering, then squatting, over the netted lids covering dhoklas or samosas, green bottle flies begging, *Let me in, just once.* I'm not sure why I like them better than regular flies, who are just as capable of feasting on a bird carcass and spreading disease—perhaps it's the bottle in the name, a green bottle, a small vessel of wind and rain packed on the back of a fly. Or is it a bottle in the throat, glistening like a metal-sheened nail polish or old and faint as verdigris on a brass candelabrum? They come, either way, through the compound gate, battling the hunger of lizards, dodging the slow blades of fans with bad capacitors, the green bottle flies. They arrive faithful as light caught in a cat's emerald eye.

Go to your safe place

Think of wild goats eating tomatoes.
Goats sharply horned and bullish.
Sucking on the luscious red.
Seeds and all. Bright in the sun.
Perhaps they're mountain goats.
Like ibexes. Where would they find
tomatoes? Suppose they did.
Tender little tomatoes with
shy green crowns over their heads.
Wild goat teeth chewing
on the red skin, all that rush
of antioxidants. All the vitamins.
Think of that.

Frogs of Bhiwandi

Pea-colored, speckled,
slobbered with
a mucilaginous green,
they fornicate behind
rusty spindles that
once looped the million threads
of a counterfeit Paithani.
For food, they lick
capsules with gelatinous shells,
slurp ovoidal fish-eggs,
snack on coin batteries
that shine like dark suns
in Amazon's basement,
and tongue some
leftover insects from
Konkan's lower plains.
The frogs of Bhiwandi
are gibbous and well-fed Buddhas,
seldom irate, except when
they must leave Thane's gates,
jump on two or three trains
and travel through Kurla,
to the notorious and most
Kopar of Ghats,
which is probably
a mistake.

In the Cow Field

It is early morning, not dawn
   yet. Pipistrelles coo from

the eaves of the cowshed.
   Eleven cows stand in a field.

It smells of dung and hay
   in the dark of the air.

I like that I am nothing to the cows
   as long as they have grass.

Ungulates so heavy,
   make me feel light.

I can't tell what's in their eyes,
   so I'm free to guess it.

The cows don't care. Whatever
   I may go on to do,

however I may stymy my fate,
   they will keep on

chewing thoughtfully
   like monks,

barely mooing, little cowbells
   cuddling their fat necks.

Fishing Cat

Suddenly, she had grown large. What she had reached the end of, she didn't know. You would think it was a pond or a lake or a brown strip of water. But what she had reached the end of was a heavy task, something like carrying an angel of stone. You might say biblical, divine. Something both brave and quiet. She didn't know what to name it. It was like water but unlike. She winnowed a pound of fish hidden in the swamp to put in her mouth, slake her thirst. She thought, how unlike me to chew their eyes. But what she had after the debacle was not a mere sign. She had stopped looking for those. What she had was large as an oceanic quake. What she had was a rumble in the earth's core. Once, all she had known was the sick bone of hunger, the thin wrist of fate. But now it grew beyond her with mass, muscle, bite, and shape. You might say divine. But what it was, was unlike a domestic angel of stone grown large in her stomach. More like birds eating birds, wild. What she had was a new appetite.

Amphibian

You can call me: anuran,   moist with semi-

permeable skin. Peptides growing on me like bees.

I was once tadpole: gilled, tailed, morphing

from frogspawn to child straight into fresh streams.

Here, see my   hindlimbs longer than my fore,

my Triassic histories more ancient than ecosystems.

We were here before you. I am sister to salamander.

I am sister   to newt.   Caecilians are my brothers:

fossorial   cylindrical serpent-bodied mysteries.

See my man   carrying   a diaphanous vocal-sac,

fluorescent,   burgeoning. Hear his old croak-song:

long & pelvic.   See   one torrential sperm release after

another. See all of these   wet   ghats in the rain.

Before the lust of your   colonization: came mine.

On Not Cleaning the Bathroom

They linger there in the damp, in the dark—
chemicals from lime-green bricks of Cinthol, blue bits of
Rin still stuck to the holes of the drain, a black tangle of
hair from three heads, carbon from the filters of ACs.
Each night a family of sewer gnats coagulates on
the broken drain cover, feasts on the quiet moisture
of the black brink. The earthworm peeks its head of string
from some epoxied gap of a cracked tile
and the millipede hungers for a spider yo-yoing
from the emptied pocket of an air-freshener.
Who am I to shake the confidence of the lizard
grown catatonic behind the bristles of a plastic broom?
Who am I to ruin the unity of things for the sake
of a sanitary impulse, the dream of a cleaner drain—
rubber pump gasping with humidity to quench
the throat of an old god, the ancient thirst
of some plumbing machine?

The Bagworm

The bagworm hangs from the cliff of wall. He hangs from the gas meter and hangs from the colander. From the udder of my eye, he hangs and drinks the moisture. Marks my cheek as an eyelash. It is tenuous, his hanging in the breeze. So tenuous I say, *Fine, you can stay with me.* So he sways from the rim of my cup, watches me drink the tea. Full of pudina and elaichi. He asks me for rotten wood, paper, and debris, so I give him the keys to my locker. He eats the house deed and licks my dead grandmother's ring, hanging from the big lock the big banker brings. Then he rides on my shoulder back to the balcony where our talk is all silence, red snakes, and fire baked within bricks. *You eat too little,* he says to break the silence, not the snakes gathering. Then crawls this way to feed me a morsel of wind. *Lick this,* he says, holding it inside the grey fold of his skin. I lick it, always with the faith of a child licking honey from her wrist. From his small hands, I drink a jug of breeze that tastes like rain, like hail pelleted on cracked earth. *Isn't it good?* he asks, now crawling up the steep road of my nose, then hanging onto the bridge of my eyeglasses. *It is good,* I nod without agreeing.

Moist

On 'moist' being listed as one of the most weird-sounding words on a list published by Bustle, 2021

I'm thinking of moist things
like moisturizers, petroleum jelly,
gooseberries,
the arms of an octopus.
Things packed with the possibility
of containing water,
icky, mucky, & beautiful,
all things viscous—
nutrient, sap, rain, resin, gum,
glowing algae in the black udder of a fountain.
I'm thinking of bogs and squelchy frogs,
squiggly waterline,
mudskipper,
skipping in and out.
Fish who drink and know what thirst is.
Swallows cruising,
swallows who make their nests
tearing clumps of wet mud
from riverbank.
Ink in the intestine of squids,
from the oviducts of sitting hens
the wonder of eggs,
great white of their albumen.
Aqueous humor in my friend's one good eye.
Damp air in wells, storm drains,
sweat in the pits,
teary-eyed statues,
moistgreen celery stalks,
dew on elephant grasses,
in the old crater of Clavius,
moonwater.

meditating on the fleas

i open the sky & in they arrive   the fleas

like guttered beings from the underside of things

they rise   fleas   out for blood

little suckers   they wrestle for life   like

roosters in a cockfight   bringing gifts

of   dirt & disease   like you wouldn't believe

in the shawls   sheets   rugs & coir mats

on the grass   where my friend T   throws

them   plucked from her dog's ears'   fur-skin

how cruel   i think   for a minute

to ruin   their feast   little parasites

from the paataal lok   alive only to become

priests of filth   then food   sustenance

for the birds   the birds   those little

flying cockroaches   sorry birds   u

beautiful bastards   twigging the blue of sky

.

The Crow Pantoum

The crow lay dead as a stone.
A dog tore away at the heart of him.
Black paw upon black crow.
The air grew rank with blood.

Tearing at the heart of crow,
the dog walked with the bird in his jowl.
The air was rank with blood.
As at a funeral, all the crows began to keen.

Walking with the bird in his jaw,
he stopped to gnaw upon the red heart.
The funerary crows keened louder.
Their black song covered the whole sky.

Gnawing on the red heart, he stopped
to look up. And then he put the bird down.
The sky was cowering with sharp black songs.
He was a good boy.

And then, looking up at the mob of black birds,
who could've told it was not a dark dream?
What a good boy he was.
And it, no dream.

Dewing

Scores of them swim unbidden
in the wettest of canals teeming
with caddisfly larvae,
smooth otter-snouts, and
amphibian affairs unknown to us.
Speaking in their secret language—
low squeaks as opposed to
the national public croak—
the frogs behave shyly
except for an occasional spa-in-the-sun
out by some rocks covered with
a green and gunky moss.
But at night, all across dark,
permeable marshes,
a million of these luminaries
anointed with a holy slime
gather at the edge of the suburbs,
which for them
is the edge of the world.
Guardians of the threshold
between water, dream,
and lung,
they begin the business of oozing
a transparent loam, something
lighter and moister than the skin of eels,
wispier than the slide of earthworms
or the oiled scalps of babies,
there in the hushed nursery
of a private waking.
In the morning,
when all alchemy liquefies
to turn common as the sky,
and the frogs return to the undergrowth
and the stalks gush with a milky sap
and the palm secretes a potful of toddy again,
all surfaces misty as the cornea of a crying eye,

nobody can tell
the secret work of dew
from the simple fact of it.

On Smelling

My one dream is to see hornbills in the wildness of sky. Their long wings flapping, warning all frugivorous trees they keep stealing berries from, and foresting the whole forest with their gold, which is to say, shit. Hornbills roll in the mud to rid themselves of ectoparasites, a behavior called dust-bathing. When their chicks hatch, the females moult and cover the tree-hollows with their faecal matter. All responsibility of feeding falls on the father bird. If he is shot for his feathers, the family is unable to survive. You can try to feed them artificially, but you will fail because body knows body and scent detects scent. When my grandfather died, he left behind his signature scent of mustard-oil on all our quilts. When we take them out during winters to sun all that smell, a shock of yellow hits our nostrils like a new death.

Rain

It is violent, this love for rain: the hail
and the haul and the pour of it
like the splatter of a thousand bombils
against a puttied drywall. It falls and falls.
Smoggy and clear. Baptizing the city's rot.
Throwing back the debris from the sea's maw.
It falls over the lonely spines of TMT bars,
over the chawls where blue sheets
of tarpaulin are weighted down by bricks,
over roofs of cars, over crows and pigs.
In the rain, all is porous, all is plain.
What mangrove. What concrete.
See the dragonflies rise heroic
from marshes, see the backhoe loaders
stuck in the mud, see the tangle of wet root
over wet root, see the skies the color
of pale mudskippers, hear the night frogs
croaking from the damp around overhead tanks.
It is beyond judgment, this rain. I stand quiet
under its muddy hoof, and like a bag of teeth
on tin roofs, it falls and falls.

Hands

It was dark as cows. But out of the tongues of frogs, the morning came. Out of the dreams of larvae and slugs, it came, shining bright as brass knuckles or the silver of fishscales. Snails dimmed their horniness and horses grew out their manes. Everything the light touched became grass, became hair. You combed the world in your small hands like a lamb's tail. Innocent. Afraid. Later, something about it would grow large and bray. Later, seasons would bald and change. Later, orchids would grow over pigswill & rot. And like a field aglow in the sun's refrain, your lit hands will comb further into the day.

Makkar Speaks

Flopping in a fishing net, I bite the nylon thread like Gajendra's leg. I bite till dawn, for a thousand days. Meanwhile, I think of the skin of fish, the plump throat of waterbirds, the slender calves of chital. Like sand coddled by turtle tracks, once the sun used to pour down my back, my scales, my scutes and snout, gentle & harsh. Now I flop all morning and then into the dimming light of the moon. I flop until the river is in spate, until the hoot of owl and the far singing of goats. I won't be prey. Bite it hard, I say. Bite the stubborn thread, like Gajendra's leg. No lotus-footed god will have his way.

ode to a toxic marsh

o sister of bog, swamp-sibling
        of squelch,
                wind beneath the horizontal hovering of
                dragonflies,
o amniotic mother
  of all larvae! i do not know
                  what it takes not to sieve, not to divide
            between smog & mist,
kin & kith, useful and useless,
        to take it all, all in.
                o superior breeder of the thin wing a
          whole family of mosquitoes
will inherit, your face
        chemical & pink-filmed
            with effluent, rainbowed with vats of toxic
            oil, microplastic blood,
slime & wet rot, o great burier
      of piscine bones!
          teach me, how to run a queendom of filth & flies, algae
              & jellied frogspawn,
a queendom so democratic
        & prosperous & long
          even the loudest of men, machines will not dare
       clean.

petition

not to let any creature's death go unlamented:
cicada, the swan with its manic beak, flamingo,
bull, turtle, badger, kite, leopard, auk.

not to let their funeral be forgotten,
to mourn, to consider them worthy
of this much. to break the locks

of all aviaries, to lure the birds out,
their beaks full of worms, not to nestle them
into something cute,

to let the wild in them remain. to beaver,
to hawk, to tree pangolin, to frog. not to let
them become tame, to recognize their frogness,

beaverhood & aukness. to respect what forms
their umwelt. to know us both as separate
and still one.

The Boar

And suddenly, he was there,
in the moonlight, dark as a fig.
A conch made out of stone,
he stood before the tall grass.
Lowering his head, he tusked
the ground for something, like
Varaha fishing out the earth
from the primordial waters.
That night, we heard no quail or owl.
Made no sound or bet.
Just stood there listening
to the beat of black hoof,
watching the light pound
on the mane off his back.
It was as if we had learned
to be newly silent. And all
the primal symbols came
back to us, rushing to our fingers
as if we had become
prehistoric women painting
the cavewalls: the ox, the toad,
the drum, the fish. And we drew
dark shapes in the wet mud
as the boar upended the earth
and we couldn't tell
the work of animal
from the work of god.

Before you go any further,

I want you to unbuckle your shoes,
walk barefoot and bend to look
into the bulk of tangled grass
to see more than a mess of green
upon green, to distinguish
wild from wild, blade from blade,
to know and to memorize
every knotted turn in the grass,
every dead snake, or a bird's
fallen jaw, not because
it's important but because
it's already so late in your life
to wait for a miracle to come
surprise you
even as you hold the very grass,
a thing so astonishingly old
its fossil was found hidden
in the teeth of some dinosaurs.

Pangolin

Like a good fist, she curls into a ball. Mad, the gush of the river. Mad, the thrall of the moon in the sky of night. Like a curlicue, she folds into herself. Inside her, a scattering of scales cutting like scythes. Like snakes. Her scales like stiff shells, adamantine. Long, the shadow of mounds in the ground. Long, the line of black tree upon black tree. Her body, a dark twirl in the moonlight. Her hunger: a long train of ants. A dream of termites. Outside, the rush of stars. Outside, the gullies of water with blind fish swimming. Toothless, her twining into a curl. Her twining into a ball. On her hands, her hands, a gift of claws.

Acoustic Enrichment

For six weeks, a group of scientists placed
an underwater loudspeaker in a desolate reef.
It played a recording of crackles, pops, snaps,
fish-grunts, & choruses. The aim was to replicate
the sonorous din of a healthy coral habitat.
To see if the fish could be lured by
an orchestrated tune resembling the reverb
of home—and perhaps, perhaps, they could
restore all such reefs dying of marine heatwaves
with the medicine of music. And so
they played the song. And they waited.
And the fish—
the fish came back to the rubble following
the sun of sounds. Lush & plural.
Just like that. Can you imagine? They swam
this way back, the damselfish. So came
back the whole community. Eaters of plant,
plankton, crustacean, other fish, all of them.
A recovery across the whole trophic guild.
And doesn't it boggle the mind that in the stone
of their ears lies hidden the coded memory
of an ambient track? Crackle, pop, snap.
A choral song of shrimp, copepod, triton,
parrotfish, wobbegong, whale. That once
the propellers are off, and the engines asleep,
in the deep aural zones of water, all creatures
await the thump of a collective drumbeat,
hair-cells waving. That we need something to
keep us well beyond the singular wreck of our
quiet groan. The constant tick of a metronome.
A lodestar. A blue concert. Something to keep us
here, tethered. A bridge. A background score
of cicadas. Faint welding. A cackle of girls
cycling down the tekdi. The static of rain falling
in low fidelities, which for some, like me,
is its own kind of home.

Dog

I stretch. I pee. I yawn the sun into being. I quarrel with the gods over the strength of my snout. Bless my muzzle, my skull, the bite of my teeth. I snarl, I breeze. Pet of Hecate. Walking the gods, I guard my territory. Low growl in the bushes. Low growl in the mudflats. I beckon what cannot be heard nor seen. I unfasten the stiffest leash and step into the wild of my becoming, the seed of my seed. I scratch, I sneeze. I sniff up the greatest of bums. I bark up the wrongest of trees. I chase the tail of sun and snatch fish from the sea. Each night, I make new music. I coo from beneath the boxes of windows. I bellow and bleat. Up in the stratosphere, up in the streets. And then I sleep my good pariah sleep.

Elephant Orifices

My beloved texts me,
asks me, *What are you doing?*

I play his soft voice in my head,
each syllable drawing me in,
like a seeker to gnosis.

But I'm looking at the long,
ancient necks of roofed turtles.

I'm wondering about the sound
of two hard carapaces clashing
like coconut shells.

I'm thinking of beetles
that light up their abdomens—
sauntering gaily into the magnificence
of elephant orifices—

How their thick, sleepy trunks must inhale
such bioluminescence,
while their grey bodies crush
a field of green grass below.

I want to reply *I love you.*
But there is just so much fauna.

What if while I'm texting him, a sangai
wanders onto some giant phumdi?
Or a jacana lays her eggs on an old lily pad?

Who will notice then, the luciferin,
churning like small star jasmines
in the moist cave of a pachyderm's nose?

Bear

It is a jungle axiom that one never can say what a bear will do.

—Dunbar Brander

So shall it be. I hang by the trunks of trees. Sloth is my ursine right. A black cloud of hide, my cover. My jaw's full of honey. I crack the earth's violent dust, its concrete. I hunt for termites. Suck in the dance of ants through the gap in my front teeth. The books all talk of mahua. Oh, do not talk to me about mahua. I eat it like a wildfruit, like a madwoman. I kill men for it, I kill women. Then I slobber and sleep. Constellate the night in my dreams. When I wake, my snout looks for nuts, roots, and berries. If you come close, I could claw you open like a star's belly emitting light on a dark, dark day. Or I could send you scurrying for shade, clutching whatever piece of bark you can tear. Or I could shamble down the dell and guzzle the breeze. Who can tell? A bear will do as a bear shall please.

Would you neigh for me?

If I whinnied you right. If I yodelled
the stars out of the sky. If I took you
as a man takes a man takes a man
takes a man. If I wakened
your dream alive. If I teased you
as the wind does the horse's mane.
If I carved you a ladder of ice.
If I octopussed your heart for all of time.
If I became as a woman becomes a man
becomes a woman. If I scissored the curtain
of night. If I believed in the dark shapes
your body makes. If I fettered you fine.

Offering

And haven't I seen this
many times before—
a fisherwoman
squatting on the footpath
at the lower end of the tekadi,
rubbing a dark paste of tobacco
in her teeth,
with a plastic tub of piscine festivities,
laying out bodies of surmai, bangda,
bombil, casually tossing away
a thin piece or two,
in a loose mercy, one to the crow
hopping and cawing around her,
one to the slobbering stray dog
with fur the color of a milky tea,
while giant buses honk,
driving shoals of children to school.
And do we not survive this way too,
each morning, receiving
a sliver of such plenitude, however
slim, small, or rotten its proportions,
however inessential the ritual,
this careless, casual
passing of things,
hand gesturing, fortuitously,
from one
to another.

A Case for Excessive Beauty

It is true and vile how I stay alive for it.
The yellow of martens,
the dark purpling of jamuns.
What I find beautiful
multiplies into its own being, grows
vast and becomes impossible to contain.
To feel all of it, alone, is such miserliness.
It shines like bells on the body of a lezim
all of it, ringing,
or glistening, I cannot decide—
image works upon image—
like the complexity of water, roots
coated with dew, their hair
a network of wet soil and mulchy capillaries
like brown spiderwork woven on a cloth of air
undulating in the earth's bed,
each individual web strung by wind or rain,
alive
in the thrum and throb of its own music.
It grows this way, the beauty, and
in the green bone of things,
my sadness dissolves and I'm struck
like a woman in sainted light
with the thwack of an epiphany.
And for a day or two,
it keeps spilling this way, the beauty,
inside and out, orange-red koi swimming calm
in the ripple of a pool-tide, and for a day
or two, I feel it all, changed
as if a small key had clicked open a small lock,
to reveal—what?
                    Something strange, new,
a wholeness, an exhilaration,
    both finite and not,
parts of me gathering
again, all the hooves
of all the horses in my breath, once

[. . .]

troubled and limp, now clopping
light as leaves
delivered by a courier of wind.

shilonda

we reached the last place
on the trail

a green
shallow stream

where the braver folk began
to immerse

whole selves into the pool
spontaneously

while true to my otherness
I sat on the edge of a rock

staring down
dipping my feet

watching something strange
glide toward me

a thin-legged spider
walking on water

like a small jesus
stopped to rest

at the still ground
of my shoe

and for a minute
I lost the voices ringing around me

my friend photographing the sun
our guide the group my family

[. . .]

the embarrassments
of my identity

and for once
I knew what my work was

to be rock

steady mushroom on lichened bark
centric eye of a katydid's flight

first pod of all larval light
present and alive

in the aliveness of an arachnid god
who had made with his brief stride

across my shoe
a kind of an altar

26

In the 1990s, diclofenac was used to treat cattle diseases. Many vultures started dropping dead after feeding on the medicated carcasses: *Gyps bengalensis, G. indicus,* and *G. tenuirostris*—they took a hit so bad that later the Parsis planned to build vulture aviaries for the traditional departure of their dead. I was born in that decade—somewhere around the confirmed end of Javan tigers. Since my birth, there are others who have gone extinct—birds, civets, rhinos. And yet, countless anurans hide in the Western Ghats. Turn this shola, peatland, lateritic plateau—and you will find a species still willing to live, shy only of the blessed grace of taxonomy. When my mother asks how I want to celebrate my birthday this year, I say, *Quietly.*

Telling the Bees

If you are not the free person you want to be, you
must find a place to tell the truth about that.
—Anne Carson

Tell a friend. Tell your mother,
if she'll listen.
Tell the frogs & the sparrows
& the shy sand-fish who vanish in the dunes.
Tell the desert fox and the desert scorpion.
Tell the kiang & the bharal.
Whisper it in the ear of a lover.
Tell the clocks on the wall
& the empty arcade at the mall.
Scream it to the skuas & the petrels.
Notify it to the breeze.
Yell it to the ghost in a ghost town
& to all its haunted automated teller machines.
Tell it to the ants, who may tell the bees.

An Encounter

Last morning, in the early hours,
I felt myself being watched

by the singular, black eye of a large crow
hung like a mussel on a black string

weighted on a branch
outside my window,

and when I looked back
I felt a tipping towards the dark

as if two hands were dipping
a tin bucket

into the black plash
of well-water.

Something both tinny and quiet
rushed inside to reach my ear,

scanning the very particle
of my soul.

Outside, the sun was starting to burn
and the birds were inspecting the sky,

but the black of crow remained
like a statue newly cast in iron,

and I remained too
for a year or maybe four.

The Toad

All night I suffer the hapless toad—
all night his low chirp against
the heat of the refrigerator.
Like god phoning me home,
he calls and calls me to himself.
What do you want, toad by the refrigerator?
My fortune, my house keys, my tarot deck?
What dark compulsions squirm about you,
my warty kin with podgy legs?
What must I do with your dark boom and ring?
Come out from under the fridge,
my familiar, my imp, my lodestar.
Let me turn you into a prince.

Hens stare me in the face

In the coop, in the stalls,
with their backs against mine,
they talk to themselves
in silent clucks.
I try to eavesdrop
on the private things
they are saying,
on the gestures
they make in the dark,
but they won't let me.
Those smart hens.
They knew
I'd talk about them.

Poem

I feel lonely
without animals

in my poems.
So I put you here:

cow, elk,
gaur, nilgai.

Come, hoof
the white space.

Tear it
with your ungulate nails.

And munch
on what's left

of this pasture
of a page.

All the places of sleep

I slept in the yellow light of the refrigerator.
In the cold boxes of pasta and bowls of broth.
I slept in the darkened treehouse, next
to the temple yard among weeping figs
& sonorous leaves. Thinking of fish, I slept
inside the pelican's gular pouch. Something
sleepy was already sleeping there. And then
I found myself in a baby's shoe, soft and padded.
I slept there too. Like water hidden in sand,
I slept in an igloo, hot as ice, cold as tongues.
I slept in a bed made of grass & soft prawns.
In the spiral of a conch, I slept my sleep.
After me, the fields slept. And the buildings
slept as their guardians did, little custodians
in uniforms with guns in their hands. The guns
slept too. And the dog slept his dreamy sleep
among the roses and their thorny stems.

ACKNOWLEDGMENTS

I thank the editors of the following journals and anthologies for including my work in their publications:

ASAP Art: "Invocation"

Count Every Breath: "Acoustic Enrichment"

Meanwhile: "what are you, an environmentalist?"

Milk Press (Poetry Society of New York): "Poem with No Dogs in It," "Poem with No [   ] in It," "The Forgetting," "The Glitch"

Poetry Northwest: "Amphibian," "On Smelling"

Singapore Unbound: "Green Bottle Flies," "Bear"

Sixth Finch: "All the places of sleep"

Strange Horizons: "In the Zoo"

SWWIM Every Day: "26"

The Bombay Literary Magazine: "Offering," "Elephant Orifices," "On Not Cleaning the Bathroom," "Dewing"

The Prose Poem: "The Bagworm"

Question of Cities: "Rain"

A Page of Thanks

Thank you to the one and only Diane Seuss for selecting my manuscript and blessing me with a generous blurb.

My sincere gratitude to Sohini Basak, consultant for this book, who besides gracing me with her fine editorial eye, asked me some fundamental questions which led to the making of a good chunk of poems included herein.

Huge, heartfelt thanks to Eleanor Berry, chair of the Barbara Stevens Poetry Book Manuscript Competition, who shepherded me through the entire publication process with her kind, attentive, and deeply responsive guidance.

A tip of the hat to my parents and my sister for letting me follow my obsessions.

Thank you to my friends Yashasvi and Kinjal for the warmth, enthusiasm, and honor of their friendship.

Thank you to everyone who believed in my work and in my book even before it was born.

ABOUT THE AUTHOR

Kunjana Parashar is a poet from Mumbai. Her poems have appeared or are forthcoming in *Poetry Northwest, Sixth Finch, The Adroit Journal,* and elsewhere. *They Gather Around Me, the Animals* is her first book. She has received the Toto Funds the Arts award and the Deepankar Khiwani Memorial Prize. She is an associate editor at *The Bombay Literary Magazine.*

About the National Federation of State Poetry Societies

The National Federation of State Poetry Societies (NFSPS) is a non-profit organization, exclusively educational and literary. Its purpose is to recognize the importance of poetry with respect to national cultural heritage. It is dedicated solely to the furtherance of poetry on the national level and serves to unite poets in the bonds of fellowship and understanding.

About the Barbara Stevens Poetry Book Manuscript Competition

This book, *They Gather Around Me, the Animals,* by Kunjana Parashar, is the 31st book published by NFSPS Press as winner of its annual Barbara Stevens Poetry Book Manuscript Competition. Every winner has been selected by a different highly reputed poet as guest judge. The judge for the 2024 competition was Diane Seuss.

Born in Indiana and raised in rural Michigan, Diane Seuss is the author of half a dozen collections of poems, most recently, *Modern Poetry,* issued by Graywolf Books in March 2024. Her previous books of poetry are *frank: sonnets* (2021), winner of the Pulitzer Prize and the National Book Critics Circle Award; *Still Life with Two Dead Peacocks and a Girl* (2018); *Four-Legged Girl* (2015), finalist for the Pulitzer Prize; *Wolf Lake, White Gown Blown Open* (2010), winner of the 2009 Juniper Prize for Poetry; and *It Blows You Hollow* (1998). Seuss earned a BA from Kalamazoo College and an MSW from Western Michigan University. She was Writer in Residence at Kalamazoo College from 1988 to 2017 and was the MacLean Distinguished Visiting Professor in the Department of English at Colorado College. She was a 2021 Guggenheim fellow and was elected to the Board of Chancellors of the Academy of American Poets in 2024.

This book manuscript competition was launched by the NFSPS in 1994 and was subsequently named for the past NFSPS president who put it on solid footing from the start with a major donation.

About Barbara Stevens

Barbara Stevens was born in 1924, in Cheshire, England, and grew up in Gloucester. Her education was interrupted by World War II. During the Blitz, she served in the Telephone Exchange Office, relaying information about enemy warplanes. She met her future husband, Murry Stevens, in Gloucester, when he was stationed there late in the war. She immigrated to the United States, and the couple was married in 1949 in Brainerd, Minnesota.

They lived for a while in Minneapolis, then moved to Sioux Falls, South Dakota, where they raised five children. While her husband worked as Treasurer and Controller of Raven Industries, Inc., Barbara Stevens was active in the local arts community. She was a supporter and practitioner of theater and visual arts, as well as poetry. Her poetry garnered numerous awards in state and national contests and was gathered in three books— *Crooked Paths, Cats Who Have Owned Me,* and *Whisper of Waves.*

Her service to fellow poets extended beyond her local community. She was President of her state poetry society and, for over 15 years, edited its annual anthology, *Pasque Petals.* She served on the NFSPS Board and held many offices, including President from 1985 to 1987.

In 1995, a year before her death from cancer, Barbara Stevens donated Raven Industries stock worth $10,000 to the then-new NFSPS poetry book manuscript competition. After paying dividends for several years, the stock was redeemed at over $17,000, helping to ensure the financial viability of the competition.

30 Years of Past Winners
of the Barbara Stevens Award

Note: Dates are the years of book publication.

Let's End This Now, by Jessica Barksdale, selected by Edward Hirsch (2024)

Petrichor, by Nancy Hengeveld, selected by Ellen Bass (2023)

Unpacking for the Journey, by Carol Clark Williams, selected by Rosemerry Wahtola Trommer (2022)

In the High Weeds, by Jennifer Hambrick, selected by Jared Smith (2021)

So Kiss Me, by John W. Coppock, selected by David Rothman (2020)

Snake Breaking Medusa Disorder, by Flower Conroy, selected by Chen Chen (2019)

Border Crossing, by Amy Schmitz, selected by Erin Belieu (2018)

A Landscape for Loss, by Erin Rodini, selected by Tony Barnstone (2017)

Midnight River, by Laura L. Hansen, selected by Bruce Dethlefsen (2016)

Beast, by Mara Adamitz Scrupe, selected by John Witte (2015)

Breaking Weather, by Betsy Hughes, selected by Glenna Holloway (2014)

Full Cry, by Lisa Ampleman, selected by Maggie Anderson (2013)

Good Reason, by Jennifer Habel, selected by Jessica Garratt (2012)

Lines from the Surgeon's Children, by Rawdon Tomlinson, selected by Lola Haskins (2011)

Come In, We're Open, by Sara Ries, selected by Ralph Burns (2010)

Bear Country, by Dana Sonnenschein, selected by Carolyne Wright (2009)

Capturing the Dead, by Daniel Nathan Terry, selected by Jeff Gundy (2008)

The Meager Life and Modest Times of Pop Thorndale, by W. T. Pfefferle, selected by Patricia Fargnoli (2007)

Harvest, by Budd Powell Mahan, selected by Lawson Fusao Inada (2006)

Aqua Curves, by Karen Braucher, selected by Peter Meinke (2005)

The Zen Piano Mover, by Jeanne Wagner, selected by Susan Carol Hauser (2004)

A Thousand Bonds: Marie Curie and the Discovery of Radium, by Eleanor Swanson, selected by Ruth Berman (2003)

The Fine Art of Postponement, by Jane Bailey, selected by Donna Salli (2002)

The Stones for a Pillow, by Diane Glancy, selected by David Sutherland (2001)

Binoculars, by Douglas Lawder, selected by Kenneth Brewer (2000)

Singing in the Key of L, by Barbra Nightingale, selected by Sue Brannan Walker (1999)

Weighted in the Balances, by Alan Birkelbach, selected by Anne Marx (1998)

Shadowless Flight, by Todd Palmer, selected by Michael Bugeja (1997)

I Have Learned Five Things, by Elaine Christensen, selected by Michael Dennis Browne (1996)

A Common Language, by Kathryn Clement, selected by David Baker (1995)

www.ingramcontent.com/pod-product-compliance
Lightning Source LLC
Chambersburg PA
CBHW051549120626
46551CB00013B/1432